Do-votions

Short, Active Devotions for the Classroom

Linda Bredehoft

CPH
SAINT LOUIS

Copyright © 1997 Concordia Publishing House
3558 S. Jefferson Avenue, St. Louis, MO 63118-3968
Manufactured in the United States of America

1　2　3　4　5　6　7　8　9　10　　06　05　04　03　02　01　00　99　98　97

Contents

Hugging Circle

Read: Mark 10:13–16

Do: Form a circle. Put your arms around one another for a group hug. Do this at any time—just say, "group hug."

Explain: One day, mothers brought their children to Jesus. They wanted Him to touch their children and bless them. Jesus knew how important it is to show love through touch, so He did as the mothers asked. Jesus' greatest demonstration of His love for us took place when He died on the cross to win us forgiveness. We can show love or affection for others when we touch them. A hug is one way to share love through touch, so hug those you love or care about often.

- **THANK** God for family and friends.
- **THANK** Jesus for His example of showing love through touch.
- **ASK** forgiveness for not showing love to others.

What Time Is It?

Read: Ecclesiastes 3:1–8

Do: Set a clock to several different times and discuss what you usually do at each time. For example, noon may mean lunchtime.

Explain: God gives us different things at different times. Some things may make us happy, such as dancing or laughing, and some may make us sad, such as dying, but our lives will probably include all of them. No matter what experience it's time for us to have, God promises to be with us *all* the time—around the clock.

- **PRAISE** God for sending Jesus to earth at the right time. He lived, died, and rose again so we can be in heaven with God when it's the right time.
- **THANK** God for always being with us.
- **ASK** God to help us spend time each day learning about and worshiping Him.

Guess Who's Coming to Dinner?

Read: Hebrews 13:1–2

Do: Ask everyone to name someone their family could invite to dinner. The person shouldn't be a friend. For example, they might invite

- a new neighbor.
- a visitor to church or a new member.
- a single or older adult.

Explain: God wants us to treat others as we want to be treated, even if we don't know them well. We witness our love for Jesus when we show love through our actions. The Holy Spirit can use our kindness to show others God's love. When others know we are kind because Jesus has been kind to us, they see the difference God makes in our lives.

- **PRAISE** God for the love He shows for us in everything He does.
- **THANK** God for the blessings He gives us to share with others.
- **ASK** God to take away our fear of showing love to others.

Washing Feet

Read: John 13:5, 12–15

Do: Wash and dry everyone's feet before reading the Bible passages.

Explain: Washing dirty feet isn't a pleasant chore, but Jesus washed His disciples' feet. His action showed how important it is to serve others. By washing His disciples' feet, Jesus teaches us about humility and about caring for others. He helps us willingly serve others in His name. When we help others, they see God at work in our lives. God's Holy Spirit can use our actions to lead others to know about God's love.

- **PRAISE** Jesus for His humble birth and death and His glorious resurrection to win us salvation and eternal life.
- **THANK** God for sending Jesus to die for our sins.
- **ASK** God to show us opportunities to serve others and reveal His love through action.

We Are God's Clay

Read: Jeremiah 18:5–6

Do: Give everyone a piece of clay or play dough. Ask them to make whatever they want. Share the sculptures.

Explain: Your sculpture is your creation. You wouldn't want someone to change it. In the same way, we are God's creations. He shapes our lives according to His perfect plan. Sometimes, though, we go against God's plan for us, such as when we disobey our parents. God wants only the best for us. When we ask, "What would Jesus do?" or read the Bible, or talk to a Christian friend or parent, God is at work to help us make good decisions. God cares so much about us that, because of Jesus, He forgives our bad decisions and reshapes our lives to fit His plan.

- **PRAISE** God for making us new creations through Baptism.
- **THANK** God for loving us enough to send Jesus to be our Savior.
- **ASK** God for guidance with any decisions.
- **ASK** forgiveness for choices that displease God.

First or Last?

Read: Mark 10:31

Do: Ask everyone to line up for a treat or to do something fun. Begin at the end so those at the back of the line go before those at the beginning. Be ready for complaints!

Explain: Sometimes we worry only about ourselves. We spend so much time trying to be first that we forget what's important. Jesus never let being first get in the way of His love for us. When He lived on earth, Jesus' first concern was to serve and help others. Jesus put our need for a Savior ahead of everything. He died to make sure we could be "first" with God. Jesus promises to help us follow His example and put others first.

- **THANK** God for His unselfish love.
- **ASK** God to help us act unselfishly and put others first.
- **ASK** forgiveness for selfish behavior.

Where's Your Treasure?

Read: Matthew 7:24–27

Do: Place a rock in a low, flat container, such as a 9" × 13" baking pan. Pour a pile of sand (sugar, flour, or salt works also) next to the rock. Put a coin on top of the rock and another on top of the sand. Slowly pour water into the pan. Watch as the coin stays on top of the rock, but the other falls into the water as the sand erodes.

Explain: The coins represent our treasures—things that are important or valuable to us. The rock represents God's love and care—our greatest treasures. The sand represents trust in something else, such as the world or ourselves. Only God is worthy of our trust. He can and does keep us safe. Anything else we trust in will fall apart. God sends His Holy Spirit to strengthen our trust in Him and live according to His Word.

- **PRAISE** God for His power. He is stronger than everything.
- **THANK** God for protecting us.
- **ASK** God to strengthen our trust in Him.

Milk ... It's Good for Us

Read: 1 Peter 2:2–3

Do: Ask what babies drink. Explain that all babies, even baby animals, drink milk. Serve milk. Compare baby pictures with pictures of older children. How have the children changed?

Explain: Milk helps babies grow strong. It strengthens the bones of older kids too. God's Word is like milk. It helps our faith grow strong. The Bible helps us grow spiritually. God brings us closer to Himself as we learn more about Him from reading and studying the Bible. Babies crave, or *really want*, milk. We can ask God's Holy Spirit to make us *really want* to read and learn about God and become spiritually strong.

- **THANK** God for His Word, the Bible, and its message that Jesus is our Savior.
- **ASK** God to open our hearts as we read or listen to the Bible.
- **ASK** forgiveness for not wanting to learn more about God.

Wrapped Packages

Read: James 2:1–4

Do: Display two gifts—one nicely wrapped and the other messy and dirty. (Be sure both gifts are the same.) Ask which gift is better and why. Open both gifts.

Explain: The two gifts looked very different on the outside, but they were the same on the inside. We couldn't tell from the wrappings which was better. We can't tell what people are like on the inside by looking at their hair, their clothes, or some other part of their body. In fact, God warns us about making decisions based on how people look on the outside. God created everyone. And God loves us so much that He sent His Son, Jesus, to redeem us. We're special to God. He helps us love others like He first loved us.

- **PRAISE** God for making everyone different. It's much more interesting.
- **ASK** forgiveness for thinking worse of someone because of how he or she looks.

We Can Trust God

Read: Psalm 37:5

Do: Pair up everyone for a trust walk. Blindfold one member of each pair. Ask the partners to lead those who are blindfolded around the room or outside. Switch roles. Ask how it felt to be blind. Ask whether they trusted their partner.

Explain: It would be pretty hard to be blind. You'd probably never be sure you were headed the right way. Our sin makes us blind. We can't see the path God wants us to walk. But God sent Jesus to walk the path for us. He straightened things out when He died to take the punishment for our sins. Because we have the gift of faith, we trust God to keep us on the right path. He promises to walk with us the whole way.

- **THANK** Jesus for walking the path to the cross.
- **ASK** God to remind us that He is leading us.
- **ASK** forgiveness for trying to walk without God.

The Classroom Altar

Read: 2 Chronicles 4:1

Do: Choose a place in the classroom to have devotions. Set up an altar. Include a cross, a Bible, candles, a favorite prayer book or hymnal, a vase for flowers, and a banner.

Explain: The temple Solomon built for the Lord included a magnificent altar. The temple itself was made from the best materials, including cedar wood and gold (2 Chronicles 3:1–4:22). Solomon loved the Lord so much that he wanted to honor God with this building. Our homes and our classroom also can be places where we honor God. Making a special area for worship here and in our homes witnesses to friends how important God is to us. It also makes devotions a special event as we gather in our place set aside to worship God.

- **PRAISE** God for His awesome power and strength that can't be contained in any building.
- **ASK** God to help us worship Him every day.

Body Parts

Read: 1 Corinthians 12:12–27

Do: Place several items of clothing into a grocery bag. Pull each item out and ask what part of the body it's for and its purpose. (For example, a belt holds up pants; earmuffs warm ears; a dress makes us look fancy; jeans and a T-shirt are for play.)

Explain: Clothing has different purposes just like the different parts of our bodies do different things. The body of Christ, the church, includes men, women, children, grandparents, and babies. Every member has different talents. Some people clean; some usher; some visit the sick or the hospitalized. Someone might type the bulletin or mow the lawn. Someone preaches. Another plays the organ. Someone else sits in the pew. All these things are important, just like the people who do them. God has given each of us something special to do for His church. What's your job?

- **THANK** God for the talents He gave us.
- **ASK** God to show us how to use our talents as part of the body of Christ.

Joy under the Sun

Read: Ecclesiastes 8:15

Do: Ask everyone to draw a picture entitled "The Best Day of My Life." Share the pictures. Ask everyone to plan a special family day. Compare the responses.

Explain: God doesn't want our lives to be sad or boring. He wants them to be fun. Why do you think He's given us so many wonderful things to enjoy on earth? God created everything and called it good. He created human beings to rule over the earth and enjoy it. God has given us special people to share our lives. While He was on earth, Jesus went to weddings and ate special dinners with His friends. Because He died for us and rose again, we get to enjoy life in heaven with God.

- **PRAISE** God for His wonderful creation.
- **THANK** God for the blessings He gives us and for sending Jesus, our Savior.
- **ASK** God to make us truly joyful.
- **ASK** God to take away our worries so we can be happy.

The Great Flood

Read: Genesis 6:1–9:17 (Spread this reading over several days. Discuss Noah's possible thoughts and feelings.)

Do: Ask everyone to draw a rainbow. Write the following on each section:

- **Remember** on the red stripe;
- **An** on the orange stripe;
- **Incredible** on the yellow stripe;
- **Noah** on the green stripe;
- **Believing** on the blue stripe;
- **Obeying** on the indigo or dark blue stripe;
- **Worshiping** on the violet or purple stripe.

Cut out and display the finished artwork.

Explain: Noah had great faith in God and did what God told him, even though he may have been scared. God sends His Holy Spirit to strengthen our faith. We trust that God will take care of us always. After all, God kept His promise to never send another flood to destroy the earth. And He kept His promise to send us a Savior—Jesus.

- **THANK** God for always taking care of us.
- **ASK** God to send His Holy Spirit to strengthen our faith.

Who Is That?

Read: John 10:27–30

Do: Before the devotion, record voices familiar to everyone, such as teachers, relatives, cartoon characters, or famous people. Play the tape and see who can identify the voices.

Explain: Jesus says that His sheep know His voice. Because we believe in Jesus, we are His sheep, but sometimes we have trouble hearing Him. The world and our sinful selves can drown out Jesus' voice. But we can ask Jesus to send the Holy Spirit to open our ears and help us listen to and follow Him. Jesus, our Good Shepherd, gave His life to save us, and He promises that no one will take His sheep—us—away from Him.

- **THANK** God for making us Jesus' sheep.
- **THANK** God for His gift of eternal life.
- **ASK** Jesus to help us hear His words and follow Him.
- **ASK** forgiveness for listening to other voices instead of to Jesus.

New Batteries

Read: Ezekiel 36:24–28

Do: Put an old battery in a flashlight. Demonstrate that the flashlight doesn't work well. Replace the old battery with a new one. Show the effect on the flashlight.

Explain: A new battery makes a huge difference. Instead of a weak, dim light, the flashlight shines brightly. The fresh battery provides more energy. When God works faith in us, He gives us new hearts. He removes our old, stone hearts and puts in new ones. God doesn't give us heart transplants, but He does give us new, clean spirits to replace our old, sinful ones. Because God's Holy Spirit is at work in us, people can see a difference in our lives. God gives us energy and power to follow Him. God's Holy Spirit helps us shine brightly.

- **PRAISE** God for the new life Jesus won for us on the cross.
- **THANK** God for loving and forgiving us even when we are slow to follow Him.
- **ASK** God to reenergize us and fill us with faith.

Stop Fighting!

Read: James 4:1–3

Do: Ask two volunteers to stage an argument as devotions begin. Tell them to act selfishly. Watch the group's reaction. Make sure you explain the argument was staged.

Explain: When we fight and quarrel, we let our old, sinful natures take control. We let selfishness rule our lives because we want something we can't have. We "fight" to get what others have. Even when we ask for something, we might not get it because we aren't asking for the right reasons. Jesus paid for our selfishness when He came to earth to win forgiveness for us. Jesus acted unselfishly as He healed people and when He went to the cross for us. Because of His death and resurrection, we have the free gift of forgiveness and eternal life.

- **PRAISE** God for His love that overcomes our selfishness.
- **THANK** God for His unselfish gift of Jesus Christ.
- **ASK** forgiveness for selfish actions.

Help!

Read: James 2:14–17

Do: Ask a volunteer to stage an injury as you begin devotions. Tell the actor you won't offer help or comfort. Ask what everyone thought when you didn't help. Make sure you explain the injury was staged.

Explain: It isn't enough to recognize someone has a problem. Because we are Christians, we try to help others. God saw our great need for help with sin. He sent His Son, Jesus, to save us. Because God loved us so much, we want to help others with our actions and with our words.

- **PRAISE** God for everything He's done for us.
- **ASK** God to show us how to help those in need.
- **ASK** forgiveness for not helping others.

We Can't See Very Well

Read: 1 Corinthians 13:12

Do: Breathe onto a mirror until it fogs up. Try to see your reflection. Give everyone a turn.

Explain: We don't know many things about God, such as what He looks like. Sometimes we don't understand events in our lives, such as getting sick. Trying to see clearly God's plan for our lives is like trying to look at our reflection in a foggy mirror. We have to trust Him to work everything out for the best. In heaven, we'll see God face to face. We'll understand clearly what He did for us throughout our lives. Now, we can ask God to send His Holy Spirit to strengthen our trust in Him.

- **PRAISE** God for His wisdom and power.
- **THANK** God for His promise of eternal life.
- **ASK** God to remove our worries about things we don't understand.

Joyful Noisemakers

Read: Psalm 33:1–3

Do: Make noisemakers from easy-to-find objects. For example:
- pour a cup of beans or rice between two paper plates and staple the plates together.
- hit two spoons together.
- scrape a pencil or pen across the teeth of a comb.
- bang on pots or pans.

Explain: God loves to be praised by those who love Him. We can make a joyful noise to the Lord by singing, playing instruments, and shouting praises to Him. God has done many wonderful things for us and given us more blessings than we can count. God's greatest gift to us is Jesus, His Son. Jesus' death to redeem us and His resurrection are the greatest reasons to praise and thank God.

- **PRAISE** God for His mighty deeds.
- **THANK** and **PRAISE** God with songs and happy noises for sending Jesus.
- **ASK** God to help us tell others why Jesus makes us so happy.

Washing Muddy Water

Read: 1 Corinthians 6:11

Do: Make an aquifer. Place pebbles in the bottom of a clear cup or jar. Cover with a layer of soil. In another cup, mix a little soil with water. Pour the muddy water into the aquifer. Watch the water soak through the soil and pebbles. The water at the bottom of the aquifer should be more clear than the water you poured in.

Explain: God created the ground to be a natural aquifer. As rainwater soaks through the soil and rocks, it's purified. Then, deep underground, it gathers in pools and rivers. We dig wells to reach this clean water. God has purified us in a way more miraculous than using an aquifer. In our Baptism, we died and rose again with Jesus. Thanks to Jesus' suffering the punishment for our sins on the cross, God washed our sins away. Now we are His children, cleansed in Jesus.

- THANK Jesus for cleansing our sin from us through His death.
- ASK forgiveness for our sins.
- ASK God to help us share His forgiveness and love with others.

Pep Rally for God

Read: Psalm 66:1–4

Do: Share cheers you've heard at sporting events. Help everyone write cheers that praise and thank God. Make signs that praise God. Hold a pep rally for God using the cheers and signs. Here is one cheer:

Two, four, six, eight—
God's love we appreciate!
One, three, five, nine—
The Lord our God is really fine!

Explain: We scream when our favorite team wins. That's how we show support and admiration. We are part of the greatest team, God's team. God is our captain, our leader. As part of God's team, we can't help shouting with joy to God and praising His awesome power and great deeds. A pep rally tells an earthly team how special it is. We tell God how great He is when we worship and praise Him at church, during devotions, or even when we pray by ourselves.

- PRAISE God for all He has done for us.
- THANK God for His blessings to us and our families.

Not Seeing Is Believing

Read: 1 Peter 1:8–9

Do: Put chocolate, pepper, garlic, cinnamon, etc., inside opaque containers. Ask volunteers to identify what's inside each container without looking inside. Ask how they knew what was inside if they couldn't see it.

Explain: Even though we can't see God with our eyes, we still love and believe in Him. We know God exists because we feel Him at work in our hearts and see Him at work in our lives. From the Bible, we learn about the things God did. He inspired the writers to record His actions, including Jesus' life, death, and resurrection. Because God sent His Holy Spirit into our hearts, we believe the Bible is true, and we believe in God.

- **PRAISE** God for showing Himself to us in the Bible.
- **ASK** God to strengthen our faith.
- **ASK** forgiveness for doubting His presence in our lives.

Something New from Something Old

Read: Ephesians 4:22–24

Do: Make scoops from two clean, plastic milk jugs by cutting away the bottom and the side opposite the handle. Use a ping pong ball, or other small ball, and the scoops to play catch.

Explain: It can be fun to recycle something old and useless into something new and useful. In our Baptism, God did much more than recycle us. He washed our sins away as we died with Jesus and rose again as new creatures—forgiven children of God. As we recycle earthly goods, we can thank God for making us new creations in Jesus.

- **THANK** God for His forgiveness and for getting rid of our old sins.
- **ASK** God to make us new people who want to serve Him.
- **ASK** forgiveness for falling back into our old lives of sin.

Very Different

Read: Romans 12:6–8

Do: Ask each person to sit sideways in front of a sheet of paper taped to a wall. Aim a bright light at the paper. Trace each person's profile on the paper with a pencil. Color the silhouettes black and compare them.

Explain: God created each of us a little different. He also gave us different talents and abilities. We don't need to be jealous of how others look or the things they can do that we can't. It would be pretty boring if God made us all exactly the same. We can ask God to help us use our talents to His glory and not to waste them. These gifts from God help us do His will.

- **PRAISE** God for the different people He created.
- **THANK** God for the talents He has given each of us.
- **ASK** forgiveness for not using our talents to God's glory.

Accidental Inventions

Read: Romans 8:28

Do: Serve ice-cream cones.

Explain: The 1904 World's Fair in St. Louis, Missouri, had many food booths. One booth sold a wafflelike food. The neighboring booth sold ice cream. When the ice-cream booth ran out of dishes, the person next door rolled a waffle into a cone to hold the ice cream. It was an instant hit. Something wonderful—the ice-cream cone—came from something bad—running out of dishes. The Bible tells us "God works for the good of those who love Him." That doesn't mean that only good things will happen to us. Sometimes bad things will happen, but God will work through them to bring us something good. Look at all the good God worked through Jesus' death!

- **PRAISE** God for working good through bad situations.
- **ASK** God to help us trust Him even when bad things happen.
- **ASK** forgiveness for wanting things our way instead of God's way.

Fingerprints

Read: 1 Corinthians 12:4–6

Do: Use an inked pad or marking pen to cover each person's fingers with ink. Carefully roll the inked fingers over a clean sheet of paper. Compare the prints.

Explain: We are alike in many ways, but we are all very different as well. Just look—our fingerprints are all different. It's the same in God's family. We are similar because God loves us all and sent Jesus to save us. We all need forgiveness. We are different too. We each have *different* talents from God to help us spread His Word. There are as many different ways to share God's love through our words and actions as there are different gifts from Him. Let's name the unique gifts God has given each of us.

- **THANK** God for making each of us unique.
- **ASK** God to help us use our talents to serve Him.

Make Something New

Read: 2 Corinthians 5:17

Do: Peel the paper off old, broken crayons. Place several in each section of a disposable muffin tin. Put the tin in a 400° oven. Watch carefully. When the crayons melt together, remove the tin. Let cool. Share the "new" crayons. (Adult supervision is a must. This could be done ahead.)

Explain: Old, broken crayons aren't pretty or useful. By melting them, we can change broken crayons into new crayons with interesting colors and shapes. Before we knew God, we were filled with sin. We were broken and ugly. At our Baptism, God changed each of us. He made us new creations. God gave us forgiveness and eternal life because of Jesus' death and resurrection. Now that we are new creatures, we have a new purpose. God helps us serve Him here on earth and share His love with others.

- **THANK** God for our new lives through Baptism.
- **ASK** God to make Himself part of our lives every day.
- **ASK** forgiveness for acting mean and hurtful toward others.

Straight Paths

Read: Proverbs 3:5–6

Do: Place a string on the floor in a wavy, mazelike pattern. Ask everyone to walk on it. Then place the string in a straight line. Ask everyone to walk on it again. Ask which was easier to do.

Explain: The crooked string was difficult to follow because it twisted and turned. The straight string was easier and less frustrating to follow. God makes our path straight and easy to follow when we trust Him. He promises to show us the right things to do and say. He does this as we study the Bible, His Word. Sometimes it's hard to do what God wants us to do, especially when people—even adults—want us to do things we know are wrong. But God always tells us clearly—lays out a straight path for us—when we listen to His Word.

- **PRAISE** God for His wisdom.
- **THANK** God for the forgiveness we have because of Jesus for the times we don't follow His path.
- **THANK** God for His Word, which shows us how to act.
- **ASK** forgiveness for not following God's path.

What Are We Afraid Of?

Read: Hebrews 13:6

Do: Ask everyone to complete the sentence, "I'm really afraid of …"

Explain: We are all afraid or worried about something. Some people are even afraid to talk about their fears! But we don't need to be afraid of anything. God has promised to always help us. Many of us fear death the most. But even death doesn't have to scare us anymore. Jesus was strong enough to defeat sin, the devil, *and* death. If He's that strong, He's more than able to protect us. He will help us defeat all our fears.

- **THANK** God for protecting us and being with us.
- **ASK** God to remind us to call on Him when we are afraid.
- **SHARE** fears privately with God and ask Him for strength.

Happy and Sad Words

Read: Proverbs 15:1

Do: Write sentences that have been said in the classroom—both uplifting and hurtful—on slips of paper. Ask everyone to choose one slip of paper. Read each sentence out loud. Ask everyone to make either a happy or sad expression to show how the sentences would make someone feel.

Explain: We often say things without thinking about how our words may make others feel. But mean or harsh words can make others angry. They also can hurt someone's feelings. Gentle or kind words make others feel good. And when we make other people feel good, we feel good too. Jesus always chose His words carefully. He'll help us do the same thing. When we use gentle words, we show others how important Jesus is to us.

- **THANK** God for His loving words in the Bible.
- **THANK** God for those who have spoken kindly to us.
- **ASK** forgiveness for using unkind or hurtful words.

Quiet Contest

Read: Proverbs 17:28

Do: Hold a contest to see how long everyone can be quiet. No one can talk or make any noise. It may be hard to determine the winner(s).

Explain: God reminds us in the Bible that being quiet often is good. When we talk without thinking, we can hurt other people's feelings. When the world gets too noisy and our lives get too busy, we can forget about God. That's a good time to sit quietly and think about everything He does for us. Even Jesus took time out from His work to spend quiet time with His Father (see Mark 1:35; 6:45–46; 14:32–42). Let's read more about being quiet: Proverbs 10:19; Ecclesiastes 3:7; Habakkuk 2:20.

- **PRAISE** God by sitting quietly and thinking about His awesome creation.
- **ASK** God to show us when to be quiet and when to say something helpful to others and pleasing to Him.

A Well-Watered Garden

Read: Isaiah 58:11

Do: Study a plant. Discuss what it needs to grow. Plant two seeds in similar containers and place them next to each other. Ask what will happen if you water one seed but not the other. Perform this experiment and watch the results.

Explain: Plants need water to grow and remain healthy. We live in a desert—a world full of sin and temptation. God is the water that keeps us alive. Through the water of Baptism, God made us His children. He planted us in His kingdom. Like rain waters a garden and strengthens the plants, God strengthens our faith every time His Word "rains" on our hearts. Instead of letting us dry up and die, God gives us everything we need to live through faith in Jesus.

- **THANK** God for Jesus' death and resurrection. Because of Jesus, we are part of God's garden.
- **ASK** God to use us to water others with His love and care.

What Do We Need?

Read: Matthew 25:34–40

Do: Send someone a treat with a note that expresses a kind thought and include a Christian message, such as "Your friend in Christ" or "I'm praying for you." For example, bake cookies for college students or prepare a casserole for someone who is housebound.

Explain: Jesus tells us that when we help others, we really help Him. When we look for opportunities to help others, we tell God thank You for helping us escape from sin. Jesus' death redeemed us from our sinful life. Believing in Christ, we are able to show love to others. When we love others for Jesus' sake, they see how special they are to God.

- **THANK** Jesus for showing us how to love.
- **ASK** God to reveal ways to help those around us.
- **ASK** forgiveness for not showing love to others.

Whiter than Snow

Read: Psalm 51:7

Do: Use laundry bleach to clean a stain.

Explain: Regular laundry soap only cleaned part of this stain. Only bleach was powerful enough to take away the whole stain. Our sins are like stains. Only Jesus is powerful enough to take away the stain of sin. His death on the cross removed the stain. Jesus' death bleached away our sins so that we are holy and clean in God's sight. Because Jesus rose again, we have the promise of eternal life with Him. What a powerful Savior!

- **THANK** God for the forgiveness we receive because of Jesus.
- **ASK** God to help us forgive others as He forgives us.

Heavenly Directions

Read: Deuteronomy 11:18–20

Do: List things we use to prevent ourselves from getting lost (for example, map, atlas, street signs, asking for directions).

Explain: The Bible is God's Word. In it, God tells us what He wants us to do. God also tells us about Jesus, our Savior. The Bible is like a road map for life. In its pages, God gives us directions for living. Our Bible reading says God's Word is so important that it should be fixed in our minds or memorized, taught to children, talked about, and even written in our homes. Let's name three things we can ask God to help us do to remember His Word.

- **THANK** God for His Word and the guidance He gives us through it.
- **THANK** God for revealing Jesus, our Savior, in the Bible.
- **ASK** God to help us as we learn and study His Word.

Footpaths

Read: Psalm 25:4–5

Do: Trace everyone's feet. At the end of the devotion, ask each person to write a prayer on his or her footprint.

Explain: Have you ever tried to walk in really deep snow? It can be hard to break a path. But if an adult walks in front of you, you can follow the path that person makes. That's what Jesus did for us when He walked on earth. He lived a perfect life in our place and then gave His life, becoming our path to heaven. Jesus also promised to send the Holy Spirit to guide us along this path as we read His Word. Isn't our God great? He gave us His Son as our path to eternal life and walks with us everywhere we go.

- **THANK** God for showing us the path of life.
- **ASK** God to help with any problems or decisions.
- **ASK** God to teach us more about Himself.

Darkness

Read: Genesis 1:3–5

Do: Take everyone into a room with no windows. Turn off the lights. Ask how it feels to be in the dark.

Explain: It's hard to imagine that the world didn't always exist. But in the beginning, there was only God. Imagine how spectacular the very first light must have been in the darkness. When we turn away from God and sin, it is as if we are living in darkness. But God worked a beautiful miracle when we were baptized. He washed away our sin, thanks to Jesus' redeeming work on the cross. God made us new creations, shining with the light of faith.

- **PRAISE** God for His creation of light and dark.
- **PRAISE** God for His gift of Jesus, our Savior from the darkness of sin.
- **ASK** forgiveness for the sins we do.

Look Up!

Read: Genesis 1:6–8

Do: Give everyone a glass of cold water. Discuss water and its uses. Go outside. Look at the sky and describe everything you see. Discuss the cloud formations.

Explain: We often don't take the time to appreciate or enjoy God's creation. But it's fun to look at the sky and the earth and all that He has created. We see something new each time we look. God thought of everything when He created the earth. He knew we'd need clouds and rain and oceans to control the weather. He planned everything so we could enjoy living here. God even planned to send Jesus to be our Savior so we could enjoy eternal life with Him in heaven.

- **PRAISE** God for His creation of land and water.
- **THANK** God for giving us water to drink and air to breathe and especially our Savior, Jesus.
- **ASK** God to keep us from polluting the air and water.

Make Some Flowers

Read: Genesis 1:9–13

Do: Draw plants and flowers on windows with tempera paint. (Use soap and water to wash off the paint.) To make "permanent" flowers, add food coloring to white glue. Draw flowers on plastic wrap with the glue. Let dry. Peel the flowers off the plastic wrap and stick them on windows.

Explain: The song "Oh, Who Can Make a Flower" reminds us that only God can create the beautiful flowers that cover the earth. Everywhere we look—even in dry deserts and underwater—God created plants. He planned how each one would reproduce—through seeds hidden inside fruit or hard shells or even in dandelion fuzz! Each flower or plant reminds us that God has a plan for us. He "planted" us here to work for Him. God sends us His Holy Spirit to help us send out seeds of Good News about Jesus to everyone we meet.

- **PRAISE** God for the beautiful plants and flowers He created.
- **THANK** God for the careful planning that went into creation.
- **ASK** God to help us spread seeds of Good News.

The Night Sky

Read: Genesis 1:14–19

Do: Display pictures of the night sky. Study the stars, planets, and other heavenly bodies. Display books about the universe. Pass out paper stars. Ask everyone to write on their star a "heavenly" place they'd like to visit. Display the stars.

Explain: Sometimes we only think about our planet. We forget about the rest of the universe. God created many heavenly bodies beside the earth. The vastness of the universe gives us an idea of how great God is. It also can remind us of how great God's love for us is. God's love is so big that He sent His only Son, Jesus, to die in our place so we can be His children. And because Jesus rose again, we will get to see God in heaven.

- **PRAISE** God for His awesome power and greatness.
- **THANK** God for the stars and planets and how our universe functions.
- **ASK** forgiveness for doubting God's ability to help us, even though we know He's all-powerful.

Creatures Everywhere

Read: Genesis 1:20–23

Do: Ask everyone to draw an underwater scene on white construction paper or typing paper with crayons. Include fish and underwater plants. Color the background blue. Wipe a thin coat of cooking oil across the paper with a cotton ball. Let dry. The pictures will appear transparent. Display as suncatchers.

Explain: God must enjoy variety. Just look at the different fish and birds He created. Each one has unique colors or features. Some can sing pretty songs or swim fast or have sharp teeth. Each is perfectly suited to the place it lives. God has given each of us unique talents too. Some of us can dance or sing or draw. Others can run fast. When we use our talents well, we praise God and thank Him for His good gifts.

- **PRAISE** and **THANK** God for the sea and sky creatures He created.
- **THANK** God for the talents He has given us.
- **ASK** forgiveness for not using our talents wisely.

Animals

Read: Genesis 1:24–2:1

Do: Ask everyone to name their favorite animal and why it's their favorite. Display books about animals.

Explain: God created the animals. God created humans to rule over the animals. This doesn't mean we can abuse or kill animals without reason. God gave us animals for food, clothing, transportation, and pleasure. The Old Testament believers used animals as sacrifices to God to express repentance for sins or thankfulness for God's mercy. We don't need to sacrifice animals. God sent Jesus to be the perfect sacrifice. His death on the cross took away our sin and earned forgiveness for us. Because Jesus lives, we'll live with Him forever in heaven.

- **PRAISE** God for the animals He created.
- **THANK** God for Jesus, the perfect sacrifice for our sins.
- **ASK** God to help us respect animals and care for them.

The Awesome Human Body

Read: Genesis 1:26–31

Do: Ask everyone to share their favorite activity. What parts of the body are used during this activity? Discuss what's good for the body and what can harm it. Display books about the body and how it works.

Explain: Our human bodies are wonderfully made. We don't completely understand how our bodies work or develop, which shows how complicated and powerful they are. Only God could create such a complex thing. But God made us differently than any other creature. He breathed into Adam the breath of life. This shows how special we are to God. In fact, we're so special, God sent Jesus to win us forgiveness on the cross. His resurrection means we'll spend eternal life in heaven with our creative God.

- **PRAISE** and **THANK** God for our bodies and abilities.
- **THANK** God for sending His angels to protect us.
- **ASK** God to help us care for our bodies and avoid things that would hurt them.

Rest

Read: Genesis 2:2–3

Do: Ask everyone to take a short nap.

Explain: God rested after creating the world. Rest is important for our bodies and minds. It gives us time to appreciate the world around us and our many blessings. It gives our bodies time to relax. Without rest, we would become sick. Do you think God rested for the same reasons we do? God gave us the gift of rest just as He gave us the gift of His creation.

- **PRAISE** God for everything He created, including rest.
- **THANK** God for the opportunity to rest and refresh ourselves.
- **ASK** God to help us spend our day of rest, Sunday, with Him.

Bible Charades

Read: Romans 15:4

Do: Play Bible charades. Take turns acting out stories or people from the Bible.

Explain: God gave us His Word to teach us more about Himself and to show us how His children should act. When we read about Abraham or Noah, we learn about faith and trust. When we read about Peter, we learn about repentance and forgiveness. When we read about Jesus, we learn about love and God's power to save. In fact, everything in the Bible is written to teach us and give us hope. As we learn more about God, our trust and hope in Him is strengthened.

- **PRAISE** God for His Word.
- **THANK** God that we can read and study the Bible.
- **ASK** God to help us learn more about Him in the Bible.

Polluted by the World

Read: Matthew 15:17–18

Do: Fill a large, clear pitcher with water. Discuss things that pollute our lives. As things are mentioned, add dirt or garbage to the pitcher.

Explain: Music, movies, and television can pollute our lives just like dirt and garbage pollute water. They can influence us to do or think things that aren't God-pleasing. What we put into ourselves affects what comes out. Because God loves us, we want love to come out. We need God's help to choose "clean" things to watch, listen to, and read. We also need God's help as we choose people to spend time with. He promises to help us make wise choices so that our actions reflect His love.

- **THANK** God for Jesus, who takes away our sins.
- **ASK** God to help us avoid things that will pollute our hearts.
- **ASK** forgiveness for wrong choices that pollute instead of build up.

What Is the Trinity?

Read: 2 Corinthians 13:14

Do: Hold up an apple, then cut it in half and hold it up again.

Explain: We talk about three persons when we talk about God: God the Father, Jesus, and the Holy Spirit. Even though there are three people, there's only one God. An apple is not a perfect picture of God, but it can help us understand the concept of three in one. We see one apple, just as God is one. When we cut the apple, we see three parts—the skin, the flesh, and the seeds. God the Father created us and cares for us. Jesus gave His life on the cross to win forgiveness for our sins. God the Holy Spirit works faith in our hearts. But we don't have three Gods—we have one God who created us, forgives us, and blesses us with saving faith.

- **PRAISE** God—Father, Son, and Holy Spirit—for His greatness.
- **THANK** God for His creation, His salvation, and the faith He gives us.

Lift Up Your Banners

Read: Psalm 20:5

Do: Make a banner from paper, felt, or burlap. Use cloth, paint, fabric paint, marking pens, or crayons to decorate it. Hang the banner above your altar or in your worship area.

Explain: Because we love God and are thankful for all He does, we want to praise Him. Banners are one way we show our love for Him and praise God for His importance in our lives. When people see our banners, they know that we love the Lord and that He is part of our lives. Banners help us witness to others all the wonderful things God has done for us.

- **PRAISE** God for His love and power.
- **THANK** God for all He has done for us.
- **ASK** God to help us tell others about His love.
- **ASK** forgiveness for hiding God's love.

The Great Outdoors

Read: Matthew 6:28–34

Do: Go on an outdoor picnic. Look at plants and flowers, small creatures, and other things created by God.

Explain: Everything God created is beautiful, including the flowers. If God cares for such delicate flowers so easily, He will certainly take great care of us. In fact, God was so concerned about us that He sent Jesus to take our punishment for sin. Because of Jesus' death and resurrection, we have nothing to fear, not even death. God promises to take care of us throughout this life and bring us to heaven with Him when we die.

- **PRAISE** God for the beautiful flowers He created.
- **THANK** God for giving us everything we need, even Jesus, our Savior.
- **ASK** God to strengthen our faith to trust Him for everything.

Light the Way

Read: Matthew 5:14–16

Do: Place a lighted flashlight inside a large paper grocery bag. (You may need to use two bags so the light won't shine through.) Ask everyone to guess what's inside the bag. As you reveal the flashlight, ask why no one could guess what was in the bag even though the flashlight was turned on.

Explain: A hidden flashlight doesn't provide much light. It should be out in the open where everyone can use its light to see. Our faith is like a light. If we hide our faith, no one will learn about God or Jesus from us. No one will see God's love in us. God sends His Holy Spirit to help us share the Good News of Jesus through our words and actions. Then our faith light shines brightly and this can help others see God's love for them in Jesus.

- PRAISE God for His gift of faith.
- ASK God to help us share the Good News of Jesus with others.
- ASK forgiveness for hiding our faith under bad words and actions.

First-Aid Kits

Read: Luke 10:25–37

Do: Assemble first-aid kits for everyone.

Explain: The Samaritan saw someone in need. He did what he could to help the man who had been beaten and robbed, even though the two men weren't friends. Our sin made us enemies of God. But He saw how sin had beaten us and He sent Jesus. Jesus suffered and died to take away our sins. His resurrection means we'll live in heaven with Him forever. Jesus' great love caused Him to help us even though we weren't His friends. Jesus will help us show love to those in need.

- THANK God for sending Jesus to defeat sin for us.
- ASK God to help us show love.
- ASK forgiveness for not helping someone in need.

Blessings Box

Read: Psalm 115:12–15

Do: Make a blessings box. Cover a box with pictures cut from magazines that show blessings, such as houses, food, friends, clothes, experiences, etc. Cut a slot in the top of the box. Ask everyone to write specific things they are thankful for on slips of paper and drop them in the box. After one week, share the blessings.

Explain: The Lord doesn't think about blessings once a year like we do. He thinks about ways to bless us every day. In fact, everything we have comes from God—our families, homes, clothes, food, and so much more. God has even blessed us with the gift of faith. He gives it to us because He loves us, not because we deserve it or earn it. How can we thank God for His many blessings?

- **THANK** God for His blessings, including the gift of faith.
- **ASK** God to make us thankful.
- **ASK** God to help us share the blessings He has given and tell others God provides all we have.

Family Album

Read: Psalm 139:13–16

Do: Ask everyone to bring in family pictures. Compare the pictures. Discuss how everyone has grown and changed.

Explain: God knew everything about us, even before we were born. Each person is "wonderfully made," one of God's very special creations. Because He planned us from the beginning and carefully chose our features and our families, we must be important to God. God valued the people He created so much that He sacrificed His only Son, Jesus, to win us salvation on the cross. We praise God for the value He places on us when we respect the life He has created, including the unborn, older adults, and those with special needs.

- **PRAISE** God for making us special.
- **THANK** God for everyone He created.
- **THANK** God for families.
- **ASK** God to help us value all people as He does.

Give God a Hand

Read: Psalm 145:16

Do: Trace everyone's hands on a large sheet of paper. Or, make handprints on cloth with paint. Discuss what hands can do. Ask each person to write a prayer on his or her handprint, asking God to help them do something nice with their hands.

Explain: We use our hands to write, clean, and play. We can use our hands to do good and bad things. The Bible talks about hands. God created our hands. He sent His Son to take the punishment for the sinful things we do with our hands. When Jesus died to save us, His *hands* were nailed to the cross. When we help someone or use our hands to do a job well, God uses our hands to share His love with others.

- **THANK** Jesus for His loving, saving hands.
- **ASK** God to use our hands to do things that please Him.
- **ASK** forgiveness for using our hands to hurt others.

God Heals

Read: Psalm 147:3

Do: Give everyone a bandage to wear as a reminder that God loves and heals them.

Explain: A bandage wraps a cut to protect it from germs while it heals. We feel better when we wear a bandage because we know nothing can hurt us. But the bandage doesn't heal us, God does. He heals our physical and spiritual wounds. God healed our worst wound when He sent Jesus to save us from the cuts of sin. Jesus let Himself be wounded on the cross when He died to win us the healing of forgiveness. Now, when we sin, God sees the wounds on Jesus' hands and feet and in His side and wraps us in His love and forgiveness so nothing can hurt us.

- **PRAISE** God for the healing of forgiveness.
- **THANK** God for helping us when we are sad or hurt.
- **ASK** God to help us tell others about His healing power.

Not a Story

Read: Galatians 1:11–12

Do: Make up a group story. The first person begins with, "Once upon a time," and everybody adds a sentence or two.

Explain: We made up the story we told. It wasn't true. We do know one story that's completely true—the story of God and His love for us that's told in the Bible. Everything we read in the Bible really happened. Even though some things seem unbelievable, we can trust God that they happened. He doesn't lie. God sent His Holy Spirit to inspire those who wrote the words that are in the Bible. That means the Bible really contains the words of God, not of human beings.

- **PRAISE** God for His true Word.
- **THANK** God for everything He teaches us in the Bible.
- **ASK** God to send His Holy Spirit to help us study and understand the Bible.
- **ASK** forgiveness for doubting the truth of God's Word.

The Right Tools

Read: Acts 20:32

Do: Display woodworking tools. Discuss each tool's job.

Explain: We use tools to build things or fix things. With the right tools, we can make wonderful things, such as furniture or homes. God's Word is a tool. It builds us up and strengthens us. When we read and learn God's Word, God's Holy Spirit works through the Word to help us build God-pleasing lives. When we share God and His Word with others, the Holy Spirit works to build up or encourage them too. God's grace, His undeserved love for us, which we learn about in the Bible, makes us part of the house of faith, built on the strongest cornerstone—Jesus, our Savior.

- **PRAISE** God for the tools of faith, including the Bible.
- **THANK** Jesus for being the cornerstone of our faith.
- **ASK** God to help us use the Bible as a tool to build up and strengthen our faith.

Happy Birthday, Jesus

Read: Luke 2:1–14

Do: Plan a birthday party for Jesus. Invite another class. Bake a cake. Decorate the classroom. Discuss gifts for Jesus.

Explain: When we celebrate Jesus' birthday, we realize that Jesus really was born as a baby in Bethlehem. The Advent season helps us prepare for Jesus' birthday and for His Second Coming. Celebrating Jesus' birth also reminds us of His perfect life, His death, and His resurrection, which won us the gifts of forgiveness and eternal life with Him in heaven. What great reasons to celebrate!

- **PRAISE** God for His amazing plan for our salvation.
- **THANK** God for His gift of Jesus Christ.
- **ASK** God to help us invite someone to celebrate Jesus' birth.
- **ASK** forgiveness for not telling others the real meaning of Christmas.

Great Smells

Read: Genesis 1:29

Do: Display herbs and spices, such as cinnamon, anise, cumin, cloves, coriander, nutmeg, mustard, dill, ginger, fennel, rosemary, oregano, and vanilla beans. Ask everyone to smell them.

Explain: God didn't just create big things such as mountains and oceans. He created many special little things that add variety to our world. Some of His smallest blessings, including herbs and spices, add flavor to our lives or provide medicines. God's blessings come in many different packages—just like we do!

- **PRAISE** God for His blessing of variety.
- **THANK** God for thinking of even small things, such as herbs and spices, that make our lives complete.
- **ASK** God to help us appreciate all that He has created.

An Unusual Easter Basket

Read: Matthew 26:17–28:10 or a full account of Jesus' passion

Do: Number seven plastic eggs and put the corresponding item and Bible verse listed below inside. Put the eggs in a basket. Open one egg each day of Holy Week.

Egg 1	cross made from sticks	John 19:16–17
Egg 2	piece of purple cloth	Mark 15:17–18
Egg 3	dice	Matthew 27:35
Egg 4	nail	Acts 2:23
Egg 5	piece of sponge	Matthew 27:48
Egg 6	pebble	Matthew 28:2
Egg 7	nothing	Matthew 28:5–6

Explain: Each day of Holy Week, read a portion of the Matthew reference or of the full account of Jesus' passion. Open the corresponding egg, read the Bible verse, and discuss the significance of the item. Emphasize that, for Christians, Jesus' death and resurrection are the most important events of His earthly life. Through His death, Jesus earned us forgiveness of sins and defeated the devil. Through His resurrection, Jesus defeated death and gave us the promise of eternal life with Him in heaven.

- **PRAISE** and **THANK** God for sending Jesus to win us forgiveness and eternal life through His death and resurrection.
- **ASK** forgiveness for our sins, which made Jesus' death necessary.

Put It Together

Read: Hebrews 12:2

Do: Cut a large cross from heavy paper or cardboard. Cut it into pieces. As everyone gathers for devotions, give each person a piece. Ask them to make something with the pieces that reminds us of what Jesus did for us.

Explain: The cross reminds us of Jesus' great love for us. He loved us so much that He died to win us forgiveness. When we "fix our eyes on Jesus," we remember the cross. We see the tremendous sacrifice Jesus made to make us His brothers and sisters. We see our loving heavenly Father, who created us and sent Jesus to redeem us from sin and death. The cross shows us the depth of God's love for us.

- **PRAISE** God for His plan of salvation.
- **THANK** Jesus for dying to save us.
- **THANK** God for the gift of eternal life.
- **ASK** Jesus to help us follow Him.
- **ASK** God to help us share the message of the cross.

Can We Build a House?

Read: Psalm 127:1

Do: Let everyone try to build a house or tower with a deck of cards.

Explain: It's pretty hopeless trying to build a house with cards. It falls with the slightest bump or breeze. It's also hopeless to live without God. He gives us the gift of forgiveness and eternal life through our faith in Jesus. He fills our lives with joy and love. If we didn't know God, our earthly lives would be sad. We wouldn't have any hope. Because God lives in our hearts, He strengthens our faith to stand against the strongest storms. We trust Him to bring us safely to heaven.

- **THANK** God for our faith.
- **ASK** God to be part of our families and homes.
- **ASK** God to show us how to share His love in our homes.
- **ASK** forgiveness for trying to live without God.

Thank You, Jesus

Read: Luke 17:11–19

Do: Ask everyone to write a thank-you note for a gift they received or for a kind deed. Deliver or mail the notes.

Explain: Our parents, friends, neighbors, and even strangers do kind things for us, but we forget to thank them. Thanking others for their kindness shows our appreciation and makes them feel good. When Jesus lived, people had problems saying thank you too. In fact, only one of the 10 men Jesus healed of leprosy returned to thank Him. God does many things for us each day. He gives us food, clothes, homes, toys, friends, family, and more. Most important, He's given us faith in Jesus, our Savior. Let's take time to thank God each day.

- **PRAISE** God for His power to heal.
- **THANK** God for His blessings, including the people who take care of us.
- **ASK** forgiveness for forgetting to say thank you to those here on earth and to God.

Praise Him!

Read: Matthew 21:1–11

Do: Sing the following stanza to the tune of "Row, Row, Row Your Boat."
Praise, praise, praise the Lord,
Praise Him every day.
He has done such mighty deeds,
His power we proclaim.

Explain: We celebrate special events or holidays such as the Fourth of July and New Year's Day with parades. On Palm Sunday, the people of Jesus' time celebrated and praised their King and Lord, Jesus, with a parade. But their parade was different. Jesus rode on a donkey, not on a fancy float. And the parade hadn't required months of planning. It happened because the people wanted to praise Jesus. Their shouts attracted others who learned about Jesus and joined the parade. When we praise God, we tell others how important He is. We praise God as we listen to His Word and ask Him to guide and bless our words and actions.

* **PRAISE** God because He is God! Let your praise show your love!

Dear Leaders, ...

Read: 1 Peter 2:13–17

Do: Ask everyone to help you write a public official. Include words of encouragement, concerns about issues, and a statement that the official is included in your prayers.

Explain: While we should follow the laws of our country and obey our leaders, we obey God and follow Him above everything. God helps us to be good citizens. He helps us show love to fellow citizens. He helps us obey our public officials and keep the laws they pass. Sometimes, though, their actions aren't God-pleasing. Sometimes the laws they pass go against God's will for our lives. That's when we need to ask God to guide us as we share our support, our concerns, and our faith with those in public office.

* **THANK** God for our country, our leaders, and our freedoms.
* **ASK** God to guide public officials as they make decisions.
* **ASK** God to fill the hearts and lives of public officials with love and concern for the country and its people.

The Heart of the Country

Read: 2 Chronicles 7:13–14

Do: Ask everyone to draw a heart. In the upper-left section, color a rectangle blue. Draw white stars in the rectangle. Alternate red and white stripes across the rest of the heart. Make the same flag design on the other side. Cut out the hearts and display them.

Explain: Many things that we do in our country and around the world aren't God-pleasing. Our sinfulness keeps us from following God's Word. Some political leaders do things or make decisions that displease God. They are sinners just like we are. But we can pray for our land and for our leaders. God will hear our prayers, and He promises to work for our good in all things. We also can thank God for allowing us to live in a nation where we are free to pray to Him publicly. Let's use our paper hearts as reminders to pray for our country and its leaders every day.

- **THANK** God for our country.
- **THANK** God for listening to our concerns.
- **ASK** God to bless the decisions our public officials make.
- **ASK** forgiveness for making poor decisions.

Painful Reminder

Read: Matthew 27:32–54

Do: Make everyone a necklace by tying a nail to a piece of string. Wear the necklaces on the Friday and Saturday before Easter as a reminder of the pain Jesus suffered.

Explain: God knew we needed forgiveness to be His children. He sent Jesus to earth to live a perfect life and to die to save us. Jesus loved us so much He willingly died on a cross to win us forgiveness. He died because He wanted to clean away our sins. When we look at our nail necklaces, we see a painful reminder of Jesus' death. We also see a joyful reminder that Jesus' death saved us and His resurrection means we'll be with Him in heaven forever.

- **THANK** God for His great love.
- **THANK** Jesus for His willing sacrifice.
- **ASK** God to help us share the Good News of Jesus' death and resurrection with others.

What Do We Look Like?

Read: Matthew 23:28

Do: Pour salt in one bowl and sugar in another. Ask everyone to tell you which bowl holds the sugar without tasting the contents. Ask why it's difficult to tell the difference.

Explain: Salt and sugar look alike. We can only tell them apart by tasting them. Christians don't look physically different than other people either. In fact, even our actions may not show we are Christians. Even though we want to follow God's will, we still sin. And those who don't believe in God can still do nice things. Only God can see who really believes in Him. He looks inside our hearts. He sees that the Holy Spirit lives there and that we believe Jesus is our Savior. Because of Jesus, we have forgiveness for the times our actions don't show others that God is most important to us.

- **ASK** God to use our words and actions to tell others about Him.
- **ASK** forgiveness for actions that don't show we are Christians.

For Me!

Read: John 3:16

Do: Ask everyone to bring a picture of themselves. Cut out paper crosses. Put each picture on a cross. Write "Jesus died for [person's name]!" on the crosses and display them. As you read John 3:16, substitute each person's name: "For God so loved [name] that He gave His one and only Son, that [if] [name] believes in Him, [name] shall not perish but have eternal life."

Explain: We know Jesus died on the cross to win forgiveness for our sins. But sometimes we don't celebrate that this is a message *just for us.* God loved *each of us* enough to send Jesus as our Savior.

- **THANK** God for His love for each person.
- **ASK** God to help us tell others that He loves them personally.
- **ASK** forgiveness for forgetting how much God loves us personally.
- **ASK** forgiveness for forgetting that Jesus died *for me.*

How Are We Growing?

Read: Luke 2:41–52

Do: Measure and record everyone's height. Describe the ways we grow: physically (height, weight); intellectually (knowledge); spiritually (knowledge of God, following His plans); socially (new friends, new activities).

Explain: As a human being, Jesus grew from a baby to a child to a man. The Bible also says "Jesus grew in wisdom and stature, and in favor with God and men." Jesus used His mind to learn and grow intellectually, just like we do. He grew physically, just like we do. And Jesus obeyed His parents and others and grew "in favor with men." Jesus also spent time listening to the teachers in the temple and asking them questions. Jesus helps us grow in our knowledge of God as we go to church or read the Bible.

- **THANK** God for helping us grow.
- **ASK** God to bless our growth.
- **ASK** God to bring us closer to Himself as we study about Him in the Bible, go to church, and talk with Him every day.

Fishing

Read: Matthew 4:18–22

Do: Cut fish from paper or cardboard. Write a name of a person who doesn't know about Jesus on each fish. Glue the fish to a string and display it. Find opportunities to share the Gospel with these people.

Explain: When Jesus called His disciples, He said He would make them "fishers of men." Jesus asked the disciples to tell others about His love, the forgiveness He offered, and the promise of eternal life. God has called us to be His disciples too. That means we are called to fish for people too. God's Holy Spirit works through the Word of God we share with others to catch them with the message of God's love in Jesus.

- **PRAISE** God for those who listen when we talk about His love.
- **THANK** God for His love, forgiveness, and the promise of eternal life.
- **ASK** God to help us tell others about Jesus.
- **ASK** forgiveness for not witnessing to those around us.

Our Temples

Read: 1 Corinthians 3:16–17

Do: Draw two human bodies (or trace around two people) on large sheets of paper. Label one body "Good" and the other "Bad." Display the bodies. Ask everyone to list good and bad things for our bodies on the appropriate shape.

Explain: God gave us our bodies. Because He loved us, He sent Jesus to save our bodies from the destruction of sin. At our Baptisms, God changed our bodies into temples where He lives. Because we belong to God, we don't want to ruin His temples. We praise and thank God for our bodies when we take care of them. We show our love for God by asking Him to help us take care of our bodies and to strengthen our faith and keep our bodies as His temples.

- **PRAISE** and **THANK** God for our wonderful, awesome bodies.
- **ASK** God to guide our choices so they may benefit our bodies.

Pack What We Need

Read: Luke 10:38–42

Do: Pack a suitcase with things for a trip (toothbrush, comb, toiletries, clothes, and a map). Display the suitcase and ask for additional suggestions. Ask what is the most important thing to pack. Add a Bible or devotion book.

Explain: Sometimes when we travel, we pack things we don't really need. We might take a coat we never use or an extra swimsuit we don't need. And we might forget some important things, such as tennis shoes or jeans or our Bibles. Martha got very upset with her sister, Mary, when Jesus came to visit them. It seems Martha felt it was more important to cook and clean than to sit and listen to Jesus as Mary was doing. Jesus reminded Martha what was most important—listening to Him.

- **PRAISE** God for His lessons for us in the Bible.
- **ASK** God to help us spend time with Him in prayer and devotions, even on trips.
- **ASK** forgiveness for forgetting to make God most important.

Calling God

Read: Psalm 145:18

Do: Display a play telephone or disconnect a real one. Ask each person to pick up the receiver and talk to God.

Explain: God invites us to call Him at any time. We can call Him if we are in trouble or happy or just because. God promises to hear us and answer our prayers for Jesus' sake. As our best friends love to hear what's going on in our lives, so God wants to hear from us. His wisdom, power, and love are greater than any friend we have here on earth. Isn't it great to know we can talk with God at any time?

- **PRAISE** God for the gift of prayer.
- **THANK** God for listening to us and answering us.
- **ASK** forgiveness for forgetting to talk to God.

Letters for the Lonely

Read: Deuteronomy 31:8

Do: Ask everyone to write a letter to someone who may be lonely. Include statements that God is their friend and is always with them.

Explain: When we feel lonely, we think no one cares about us. We feel like we aren't important. But God is always with us. He is always ready to show us how important we are to Him. God sent His Holy Spirit to work faith in our hearts when we were all alone in our sin. Through our Baptisms, God made us part of His big family. We will never be alone again. Jesus, our best friend, promises to walk beside us all the way to heaven. What a wonderful message of love and friendship we have to share with the lonely!

- **THANK** God for friends and family.
- **ASK** God to help us tell others about His love and offer of friendship.
- **ASK** God to remind us that we don't have to be sad or lonely. Jesus is our best friend, and He's always with us.

Vine and Branches

Read: John 15:1–8

Do: Display a healthy plant. Ask what it needs to grow. Cut off a leaf or branch. Ask what will happen to the piece that has been cut off.

Explain: Jesus compared our relationship with Him to the relationship between a vine and its branches. The branches won't grow if they're cut off from the main vine. They won't get nourishment from the vine, and they'll weaken and die. We can't remain spiritually healthy and strong if we cut ourselves off from Jesus. We will weaken and die spiritually. Jesus gives us His strength, His forgiveness, and His spiritual nourishment through His Word and the sacraments. Through God's gift of faith, we are joined to Jesus and receive the promise of eternal life in heaven—and a joyful life on earth.

- **THANK** God for giving us all we need to grow spiritually.
- **ASK** God to remind us of our need for Jesus.
- **ASK** forgiveness for trying to cut ourselves off from Jesus.

The Name Game

Do: Display the items listed below. Ask what these objects have in common. Read the following Bible passages. Ask for other names for Jesus.

Light—John 8:12

Rock—1 Corinthians 10:4

Lamb (of God)—John 1:29

Door—John 10:9

Bread of Life—John 6:35

Vine—John 15:1

Gate—John 10:7

Good Shepherd—John 10:11

Explain: The Bible compares Jesus (and God) to many different things. A name such as Vine or Door explains what Jesus does for us. He strengthens our faith, and He is the way to heaven. A name such as Good Shepherd teaches us about how Jesus treats us—kindly, with love and concern. God's Word helps us learn more about Jesus and His love for us. And the different names for Jesus show us the many ways He is at work in our lives.

- **PRAISE** Jesus for His different names.
- **THANK** Jesus for being our Light, our Good Shepherd, etc.
- **THANK** God for His Word and what He teaches us in it.

Controlling Our Anger

Read: James 1:19–20

Do: Make a graffiti board. Ask everyone to write their ending to the sentence, "It makes me angry when ..." on a large sheet of paper. (Record situations, not people, that cause anger.) Discuss the list. Brainstorm positive ways to handle the situations, such as avoiding the situations, writing down feelings, or talking to the people involved. Discuss both positive and negative ways to handle anger.

Explain: Sometimes it's okay to get angry—even God gets angry at sin. But our anger can easily lead us to do sinful things. We handle anger properly when we ask God to help us avoid situations that make us angry for the wrong reason. We also can learn to think before we speak, which might help other people avoid becoming angry with us. When we ask God to help us remain calm, we demonstrate to others that God is in charge of our lives, not our anger.

- THANK God for forgiving our sinful angry outbursts.
- ASK God to help us control our temper and learn to forgive others as He forgave us.

Overflowing Blessings

Read: Luke 6:38

Do: Display two tablespoons of baking soda and two tablespoons of white distilled vinegar. Place an 8-ounce glass in front of you. Ask if the glass will be large enough to hold the baking soda and the vinegar. Pour the baking soda into the glass. Add the vinegar. It will overflow the glass.

Explain: Often we think we don't have enough. We don't recognize our blessings, or we don't think God has given us everything we need. The baking soda and vinegar seemed small compared to the size of the glass, but combined, they more than filled the glass. That's how God's blessings are. God promises to give us everything we need. In fact, He gives us so much, we aren't aware of it all. Because God is so generous, we can be generous to others. What He has given us overflows into the lives of others.

- THANK God for our blessings.
- ASK God to make us truly thankful.
- ASK God to teach us how to share our blessings freely.

Watch What We Say

Read: Ephesians 4:29

Do: Loosely and gently place a piece of tape over every one's mouth.

Explain: We often say things without thinking. These words can be hurtful or mean. Instead of bringing God glory, our words show we are sinners. But God forgives our hurtful words and helps us speak words that encourage and make others feel good. We can picture our mouths covered with invisible spiritual tape so that we remember to ask God to guide our words so they build up others instead of tear them down.

- **THANK** God for kind words from others and for His words of love in the Bible.
- **ASK** God to help us say things that build up other people.
- **ASK** forgiveness for saying hurtful things.

Keep It Lit

Read: Matthew 5:14–16

Do: Light a candle. Place it under a clear glass jar or bowl. Observe what happens.

Explain: Our candle went out because it didn't have enough oxygen to keep burning. Jesus asks us to share the good news about His death and resurrection. Jesus even calls us lights to the world. When we don't tell others about Jesus, it's like hiding our light. We hide Jesus. When we cover up our faith, it's like lighting a lamp but not using it. And if we cover it up, we probably aren't paying attention to our faith. That means we aren't feeding it with God's Word. It's in danger of going out, just like the candle when it was separated from the oxygen. We can ask God to keep us shining brightly for others. He will strengthen our faith and keep us glowing so others will know how great He is.

- **THANK** God for lighting the lamp of faith in our hearts.
- **ASK** God to use us to light the way to Him for other people.

Me and My House

Read: Joshua 24:15b

Do: Ask everyone to draw a picture of their house on a small piece of heavy cardboard. Ask everyone to identify one thing they really like about their house (neighbors, their bedroom, a favorite decoration, a favorite hiding place). Cut out the houses and glue on magnets. Write Joshua 24:15b on the front.

Explain: Your parents probably display your artwork or your grades on the refrigerator. They also might have family snapshots turned into refrigerator magnets. But do these items show that you and your family serve the Lord? When Joshua brought the Israelites into the Promised Land, they dedicated their homes and their lives to God. Ask God to help you honor Him in all that your family does. Display your refrigerator magnet as a symbol that you and your family love and serve God.

- **THANK** God for our homes and families.
- **ASK** God to be the center of our homes.
- **ASK** God to guide our families' actions.
- **ASK** God to remind us to have family devotions and prayers.

What? No Lights?

Read: Psalm 119:105

Do: Ask a volunteer to solve a math problem, draw a picture, or sweep the floor. As the person begins, turn off the lights and close the shades. The person must complete the task in the dark. If they object, ask why. Discuss how light makes things easier to do.

Explain: The task I gave [name], couldn't be done without light. We need light to see properly. When it's dark, we can't focus correctly, and it becomes difficult to complete our tasks. God's Word is a light. It shows us the path God has laid out for us. The Bible shows us how to act, and it shows us our Savior, Jesus. Without God's Word, we'd be walking blind, trying to get to heaven on our own. Because God inspired the writers to record His Word, we know Jesus lights the way to heaven for us.

- **THANK** God for His Word.
- **THANK** Jesus for lighting the way to heaven.
- **ASK** God to help us see His guidance through our parents and teachers.

In a Nutshell

Read: John 3:16

Do: Give everyone a peanut. Help those who haven't already done so memorize John 3:16.

Explain: We call John 3:16 the Gospel in a nutshell because it's a simple way to explain God's love. And it clearly says that God sent Jesus to be our Savior. Because we believe this, we'll go to heaven. What an important passage to remember and always be ready to share with others! You can hang on to the peanut as a reminder of John 3:16—the Gospel in a nutshell—and of God's great love.

- **PRAISE** God for His plan of salvation.
- **THANK** God for sending Jesus to die and rise again to win us forgiveness and eternal life.
- **ASK** God to help us remember John 3:16 and share its message with others.

Jesus in My Pocket

Read: John 14:27

Do: Cut out paper hearts. Write *Jesus* on them. Give several to everyone to put in their pockets, drawers, desks, etc. Ask what gives peace.

Explain: Some people think strong armies bring peace. Some think a paper signed by world leaders brings peace. I feel peaceful when I listen to music. But there's only one person who gives us real peace. That's Jesus. Because the Holy Spirit has worked faith in our hearts, we receive many gifts, including eternal life and forgiveness. But Jesus also promised to give us His peace. We have peace because we know Jesus is always with us, watching out for us and helping us follow Him. We don't have to worry about anything, even death. Let's carry these paper hearts to remind us of Jesus' constant presence and His gift of peace.

- **PRAISE** Jesus for His gift of peace.
- **THANK** Jesus for taking care of our worries.
- **ASK** Jesus to increase His peace in us when we are worried or afraid.
- **ASK** forgiveness for doubting Jesus can help us.

My Rock

Read: Psalm 18:2

Do: Write "Jesus is my rock" with paint or marking pens on a rock for everyone. Ask them to place the rocks outside their houses.

Explain: Rocks are strong. It takes a lot of power to break them. They don't rot. They aren't easily moved. Homes built from rocks are sturdy and safe. God is our rock. He is the strongest. He can protect us from anything. He won't leave us or fall apart when the going gets tough. We can count on Him to always love and protect us. God even moved the rock from in front of Jesus' tomb. This shows us that Jesus defeated sin, death, and the devil through His death and resurrection and won for us forgiveness and eternal life.

- **PRAISE** God for His strength and power.
- **THANK** God for His love and protection.
- **ASK** God to increase our trust in Him.
- **ASK** forgiveness for doubting God's power, strength, or love.

Hidden Love in Action

Read: Matthew 6:1–4

Do: Wrap a shoebox. Cut a slot in the top. Paste hearts on the box. Ask everyone to plan and do in secret an act of love for a family member, a classmate, or a teacher. Ask them to cut out a heart, write their deed on it, and put it in the box. At week's end, thank God for the acts of love, but don't share what was actually done.

Explain: Sometimes we do good things so everyone can see how great we are. We want to be praised. That's not how Jesus said we should do good things. He said our acts of love should bring praise to God and show others how great He is. When we show love to others because God first loved us, God's Holy Spirit is working in us. He blesses our words and actions so they witness to others how important God is to us.

- **THANK** Jesus for His loving actions for us, including His death and resurrection.
- **ASK** God to help us show love to others.
- **ASK** forgiveness for showing off instead of pointing to God.

Powered by the Holy Spirit

Read: Romans 8:9

Do: Draw a train engine on a sheet of paper. Write "Powered by the Holy Spirit" on it. Ask everyone to draw a train car on a sheet of paper and describe a loving action that could be performed for a friend, a family member, or a stranger. Attach the cars to the engine.

Explain: A train engine provides the power to move a train. The train can't get anywhere without it. God sent His Holy Spirit in our Baptism to work faith in our hearts to believe in Jesus. The Holy Spirit makes us able to do good deeds, to "move" for Jesus. Without the Spirit's power, we could do nothing. With His help, we share Jesus' love when we tell others that Jesus is our Savior.

- **THANK** God for His gift of the Holy Spirit.
- **ASK** God to send His Holy Spirit through His Word to empower us to "move" for Jesus.

Where's Our Treasure?

Read: Matthew 6:19–21

Do: Ask everyone to complete the sentence, "The most valuable thing I have is …" Discuss the items mentioned. Ask whether those valuables could be lost or destroyed.

Explain: We each collect something. Maybe it's baseball cards or rocks or postcards. No matter how well we take care of our collections, they won't last forever. Toys, clothing, cars, even people, get broken, stolen, worn out, or lost. Eventually, earthly items will be gone forever. What won't be destroyed? Heaven can't be destroyed. God promises that nothing can separate us from Him. We will last forever because God has promised to take all believers to heaven.

- **THANK** God for His everlasting love.
- **ASK** God to help us treasure His love.
- **ASK** forgiveness for placing earthly things ahead of heavenly things.

Family Prayers

Read: Ephesians 6:18

Do: Make a family prayer book. Ask everyone to bring a family picture. Place them in an album or mount them on paper. Write the family members' names beneath the photos. Use the book each day to pray for a different family.

Explain: God has given us prayer as an important part of our Christian life. When we talk to God, we share our lives with Him and trust that He will answer our prayers. Establishing a prayer routine may keep us from only praying when we're in trouble. Instead, we'll pray every day, in good times and bad. One way to establish a prayer routine is to make a prayer book. Our family prayer book will remind us of the people we love and of their special needs. Then we can bring each person before God and ask Him to bless them and keep them close to Him. God invites us to pray all the time. He will always listen and answer our prayers for Jesus' sake.

- **THANK** God for families and all who are special to us.
- **ASK** God to remind us to pray every day.

Special Me!

Read: Romans 1:1

Do: Ask everyone to name things they like about themselves (a physical trait, a talent, etc.).

Explain: God created each of us special and unique. When God's Holy Spirit worked faith in us at our Baptisms, God made us even more special. He also gave us unique gifts. Paul writes that as Christ's servant, he was "called to be an apostle." He even writes that God set him apart for this job. Paul must have been very special to God to be set apart to tell others about Jesus. But God has set each of us apart too. We each have a special gift or talent that will help us share Jesus with others. Isn't it awesome to know God thinks we're each special?

- **THANK** God for our unique talents and abilities.
- **ASK** God to help us use our gifts to His glory.
- **ASK** forgiveness for our complaints or ungrateful attitudes when we compare what we have with others.

Plugged In and Turned On

Read: 1 John 3:18

Do: Display a small appliance, such as a hand mixer or blender. Attempt to make it work. Ask why it isn't working. After you plug it into an electrical outlet, ask why it still won't work. Agree that you need to turn it on.

Explain: Just like our mixer [blender] needed electricity to work, we need God. God empowers us to truly live a joy-filled life. When God's Holy Spirit plugs us into His Word, we learn how to live His way. The Holy Spirit gives us the power to follow Jesus. But just being plugged in isn't enough. Our good works, which we do by the Holy Spirit's power, show others that God is the power in our lives. We get turned on and do things for God because God is part of our lives.

- **THANK** God for His power in our lives.
- **ASK** God to help us show love for others.

Popcorn and the Gospel

Read: Isaiah 63:7

Do: Pop popcorn.

Explain: How does popcorn explode? I read that the kernels explode because they get so hot that they have to blow up. We are like popcorn. The Good News about Jesus is so exciting that it fills us with joy. We get so full of joy that we have to explode in loving words and actions. Just as popcorn gets so hot it has to explode, we can be excited witnesses for Christ to everyone we see.

- **PRAISE** God for His saving love.
- **THANK** Jesus for winning us salvation from our sins.
- **ASK** God to help us witness the joy and excitement of His love and salvation to others.

Get Away, Devil!

Read: Matthew 4:1–11

Do: Fill a bowl with water. Sprinkle pepper on top of the water. Dip one corner of a bar of soap in the peppered area. Watch closely. Discuss what happened.

Explain: The water represents us. The pepper represents sin and the devil. When the devil tempts us to sin, it makes a mess of our lives, like the pepper messes up the water. Only God can clean things up. God is so powerful, He makes the devil run away, like the soap moves the pepper. When Jesus was tempted by the devil, He didn't fight the devil on His own. He quoted God's Word. The devil couldn't avoid the truth of God's Word. He lost. Jesus won. Because Jesus defeated sin, death, and the devil on the cross and in His resurrection, we can tell the devil to get away. Jesus beat him for us.

- **PRAISE** God for His awesome power.
- **THANK** Jesus for defeating the devil when He died to win us forgiveness.
- **ASK** God to help us resist temptation to sin.

ABC Thanksgiving

Read: Psalm 100:4

Do: Ask everyone to name something for which they are thankful. Each item should begin with a different letter of the alphabet, beginning with the letter A. (For example, "I thank God for **a**pples." "I thank God for my **b**aseball team." "I thank God for **c**ars.")

Explain: God deserves thanks and praise for all that He has created and for the gifts He gives us. Everything that improves our lives—such as cars, computers, and machines—is really a gift from God. Food, clothes, homes, and families come from God too. What tremendous love He must have for us to be so generous! But God's greatest gift came in a very small package—Jesus, born as a baby to be our Savior. His death and resurrection won us the gifts of forgiveness and eternal life with God forever in heaven.

- **PRAISE** God for His many gifts, especially for Jesus.
- **THANK** God for something extra special.
- **ASK** forgiveness for our ungrateful attitudes.

Don't Forget!

Read: Isaiah 49:15

Do: Put 10 to 15 items on a table. Cover them with a cloth. Display the items for one minute. Cover them again. Tell everyone to write down as many items as they can remember.

Explain: Some of us have good memories—you could name all the items. Others could only remember a few. God never forgets His people. He knows the name of every person who has ever lived. And He knows the name of every person who will be born. That's amazing. We sometimes forget about God. We forget to follow His path. We even forget to share God with others. We sin. But God's perfect memory won't let Him forget us. He sends His Holy Spirit through His Word to remind us of Him. He shows us our need for forgiveness, and then God gives us forgiveness for Jesus' sake.

- **THANK** God for remembering us and forgiving us.
- **ASK** God to remind us to forgive others and share the Good News of Jesus with them.

God Loves Me!

Read: 1 John 4:7–11

Do: Let each person look in a mirror and say, "God loves me."

Explain: We use the word *love* a lot. Sometimes we use it to describe people we *like*, not love. When we really love someone, we're willing to do anything for him or her. A good example of love is a parent who will sacrifice his or her own life to save the life of the child. But we have an even better example of love. We have God. He loved us so much that He sent His only Son, Jesus, to earth to live, suffer, and die to win us forgiveness. Then God raised Him from the dead so we could have eternal life. God loves us so much that He has made us His own children through Baptism. Isn't His love amazing?

- **THANK** God for His great love.
- **THANK** God for sending Jesus to save us. What a loving act!
- **ASK** God to use us to show His love to others.

You're Nice

Read: Psalm 19:14

Do: Ask everyone to say something positive and sincere about one other person.

Explain: How do you feel when someone says something nice to you? How about when someone says something mean? When we take control of our words and actions, we sometimes say things that hurt. But when God controls our words and actions, He uses us to show His love to others. God loved us enough to send Jesus to earn forgiveness for the times we say mean things. He promises to give us His power to help us say loving things to others.

- **THANK** God for the special people in our lives.
- **ASK** God to help us say kind things to others.
- **ASK** forgiveness for the mean things we say or do to others.

Dial Direct

Read: Proverbs 11:13

Do: Play telephone. Start a message by whispering a sentence or phrase into the ear of the person sitting next to you. That person whispers it into the next person's ear and so on. The last person in line says the message out loud. Compare it to your original message.

Explain: Just like our message got confused the further it got from me, news about other people gets confused when it's repeated. Jesus says we should talk directly to the person we have a problem with. Then we can work together to find a solution. If we talk behind people's backs, we tear them down instead of build them up. We can ask Jesus to guide our words and actions and help us talk directly to people when we have problems or concerns. He has won us forgiveness for the times we do gossip.

- **THANK** God for dealing directly with our sins by sending Jesus as our Savior.
- **ASK** God to help us avoid gossip.
- **ASK** forgiveness for gossiping.

A New Creation

Read: 2 Corinthians 5:17

Do: Pour whipping cream into a glass jar with a tight-fitting lid. Ask everyone to take turns shaking the jar for one minute until a solid mass forms. You've made butter. Serve the butter with crackers.

Explain: When God sends His Holy Spirit to work faith in our hearts, we become new creations. God changes the sinful people we were into His precious sons and daughters. Jesus' suffering, death, and resurrection save us from our sins and give us the gift of eternal life in heaven with Him. God's gift of salvation makes us different people, just like the cream was turned into butter.

- **PRAISE** God for His gift of faith.
- **THANK** God for sending Jesus to win us salvation.
- **ASK** God to help us tell others about our new life through Jesus.

Thank You, God

Read: Hosea 6:3

Do: Ask someone to look up *acknowledge* in a dictionary. Discuss the meaning of the word, focusing on "making known what one has received." On a sheet of paper or on the chalkboard, write a group thank-You note to God. Ask everyone to write a personal thank-You note to God.

Explain: When a school or museum receives a special gift, it holds a special ceremony to *acknowledge* the gift and the donor. We've received something much greater than money or artwork. God has given us our life, our faith, and our Savior. He's also given us everything we need to live on earth. God deserves our *acknowledgment,* or our thank-Yous, for all He does for us.

- **THANK** God for His blessings and actions on our behalf.
- **ASK** God to help us praise and thank Him in all we do.
- **ASK** forgiveness for forgetting to acknowledge God for His gifts.

Snowflakes

Read: Jeremiah 29:11–12

Do: Fold a sheet of white paper to make a snowflake. Tell everyone the paper represents a person. Ask everyone to name one difficult time (a time they were scared, sad, hurt, worried, etc.). Cut a notch in the paper for each experience. Reveal the snowflake.

Explain: Our fears, trials, and worries can eat away at us. They make us feel out of control and afraid. We feel incomplete, not good enough. We can't make it alone. But God has a plan for our lives. He will take away our fears and worries and use our trials for our good. Through the gift of faith, He makes our lives beautiful. Just like snowflakes are unique and beautiful, so our lives are unique and beautiful. God helps us overcome our weaknesses by getting rid of our worries with His love, strength, and forgiveness.

- **PRAISE** God for His plan for our lives.
- **ASK** God to help us overcome our fears and get rid of our worries.

Imitators of God

Read: Ephesians 5:1–2

Do: Play Simon says.

Explain: In the game, we imitate—or do—what the leader says. In life, we are to imitate God. But God knew we couldn't do what He asks on our own. That's why He sent Jesus to win us salvation. Then God worked faith in our hearts at our Baptisms. The Holy Spirit now lives in us and helps us follow Jesus' example. The Holy Spirit helps us love others as Christ loved us and gave His life to win us forgiveness.

- **PRAISE** God for His great love.
- **THANK** God for sending Jesus to save us.
- **ASK** Jesus to help us imitate Him.
- **ASK** God's help to tell others about His love.

How Many Hairs?

Read: Matthew 10:29–31

Do: Ask two volunteers to count the hairs on your head. When they give up, ask if anyone knows how many hairs the average human has (about 100,000).

Explain: If God knows how many hairs we have, wouldn't He know other, more important things about us? Wouldn't He know that we are afraid of thunderstorms? Wouldn't He know that we play the piano well? God knows everything about us because He created us. He cares about what happens to us. God sends His Holy Spirit through His Word to help us trust and love Him. When we trust and love God, we know that He will lead us to make the right choices in our lives. We don't need to worry or be afraid of any decision or any problem. God will always take care of us.

- **THANK** God for knowing everything about us, especially that we needed a Savior.
- **ASK** God for help with any worries or concerns.
- **ASK** forgiveness for not turning worries over to God.

Good Habits

Read: Hebrews 5:13

Do: Brush your teeth. Why is it important to brush our teeth? How often should we brush them? What else can we do to keep our teeth strong?

Explain: When we take care of our teeth, we make sure we'll have them for a long time. If we forget to brush or floss, our teeth may rot and fall out. We keep our teeth strong when we brush and floss and visit our dentist. It's also important to take care of our spiritual health. Our faith is kept strong by God as we study His Word, spend time learning about Him, and worship Him. Developing good spiritual habits is more essential than developing good dental habits. God's Holy Spirit works through His Word to nourish our faith and keep us healthy members of Christ's body.

- **THANK** God for the gift of His Word.
- **ASK** God to help us develop good spiritual habits.
- **ASK** God's Holy Spirit to nourish us as we read the Bible.

Beloved Birds

Read: Matthew 6:25–26

Do: Make a birdfeeder. Cut the side from a clean, plastic milk jug. Fill it with birdseed. Hang it in a tree. Or, spread peanut butter on a slice of bread or on a pinecone. Coat the peanut butter with birdseed or oatmeal. Hang the pinecone or bread from a tree limb or lay it on the ground where birds can eat from it.

Explain: God cares for even the little sparrows that He created. If He cares about a small animal, just think how much He must care about and love us—the people He created in His image. We're so special, God sent His only Son, Jesus, to redeem us from sin, death, and the devil. We celebrate God's great love when we show love to others through our words and actions. We even thank God for loving us when we love the animals He created. Even a birdfeeder can show God how thankful we are that He cares for and loves us.

- **THANK** God for caring about us and all creatures.
- **ASK** God to help us care for others, even animals.

Bubbles and Roots

Read: Ephesians 4:14–16

Do: Blow bubbles outside. Walk to a large tree. Ask everyone to blow on it—or push, pull, and tug it.

Explain: Why does the wind move bubbles so easily, but we can't make this tree move at all? One reason is the bubbles aren't attached to anything. The tree, however, has strong roots holding it firmly in the ground. Even if you cut it down, removing the tree's roots would take a lot of work. As Christians, we "grow up into" Christ. As God's Holy Spirit teaches us more about Christ from God's Word and strengthens us, we are rooted more firmly in Christ. We won't be easily confused by false things other people tell us. When we're rooted in Christ, we won't wander around like bubbles.

- **ASK** God to keep you rooted in Christ.

Follow Our Leader

Read: 2 John 1:6

Do: Play follow the leader. Discuss who we are to follow as we walk through life. Who shows us what to do and how to act? Where can we find out more about this person?

Explain: It can be difficult to follow when the leader does something we can't. Jesus says we are to follow Him. But we can't follow Him by ourselves. God took care of that problem by sending His Holy Spirit to give us faith. Our faith puts us on the path with Jesus. He died for us on the cross. He died to take the punishment for our sins. And He rose to give us the gift of eternal life. Now Jesus walks the path to heaven with us, showing us how to love others as He loved us.

- **PRAISE** God for the life of love Jesus led.
- **THANK** God for His love shown in His gift of Jesus.
- **ASK** God to help us show love in all that we do.

A Blessing Tree

Read: Psalm 106:1

Do: Make a blessing tree. Draw a tree on a sheet of paper or on a bulletin board. Do not draw leaves. Ask everyone to draw a leaf on the tree (or cut one from paper) and write one thing on it for which they are thankful. Each person can add as many leaves as they want. Watch the tree fill up quickly with blessings!

Explain: God has blessed us in many ways. He's given us life and health, food and clothing, family and friends, and all our possessions. We have so much that we can't begin to remember it all. Most important, God sent Jesus to die and rise again to win us forgiveness and eternal life. And He's given us the gift of faith in Jesus. As we add leaves to our blessing tree, let's each include a leaf for Jesus and another for our gift of faith.

- **PRAISE** God for His everlasting love.
- **THANK** God for His good gifts.
- **ASK** God to guide us as we share our blessings and His love.

And It Was Very Good!

Read: Genesis 1:31

Do: Display materials on recycling, energy conservation, and other environmental issues. Ask the group to choose a conservation method to apply in the classroom, such as recycling; turning the thermostat up/down two degrees; sponsoring a "No Trash" lunch day when reusable containers and cloth napkins are used; turning off unnecessary lights; planning a neighborhood/ school cleanup; planning a paper/aluminum drive.

Explain: The world God created was perfect. Even today, we can still see His awesome power and wisdom in nature. However, we spoil or destroy nature in many ways, including when we pollute our environment with waste products. We can do our part to reduce the amount of garbage we make in our homes and classroom. God created a beautiful world for us. We do our part to respect His creation when we respect life, keep our surroundings clean, and educate and encourage others to do the same.

- **PRAISE** and **THANK** God for His marvelous creation.
- **THANK** God for sending Jesus to clean our polluted lives.
- **ASK** forgiveness for polluting God's world.

School Walk

Read: Deuteronomy 6:6–9

Do: Take everyone on a walk through the school. List the items in each room that show Christians are there (for example, crosses, Bibles, and pictures of Jesus). List the rooms that don't display something about God. What could be added to show Christ lives in that room? What could be added outside the school to reveal Christ?

Explain: God is present when we work, play, study, sleep, and eat. Sometimes we forget He's always watching. The devil tempts us to disobey our teachers or say something mean to a friend. God's Holy Spirit may use a reminder of God that's around us, such as Jesus' picture or a cross or a Bible, to urge us to follow Jesus' example. These items also witness to others God's importance to us.

- **PRAISE** God for being a part of our school and for loving us.
- **ASK** God to make our school a witness to His great love.
- **ASK** forgiveness for not following Jesus' example.

Workers for the Lord

Read: Acts 1:8

Do: Display pictures of various professions (for example, pastor, construction worker, nurse, salesperson, teacher, police officer, etc.). Ask which worker serves God more.

Explain: Does one profession really serve God more than another? Jesus has called each of us to be His witnesses. God has given us unique talents to use as we witness to others. When we do our work for God, whether it's nursing or typing or preaching, we show others what God has done for us. No matter what we do when we grow up, or even now while we're in school, God will use us to bless others.

- **THANK** God for the talents He has given us.
- **ASK** God to help us share His love in everything we do.
- **ASK** forgiveness for not appreciating or using our talents.

No Luck

Read: Romans 8:28

Do: Discuss symbols that are associated with being lucky or unlucky, St. Patrick's Day, or superstitions (for example, rabbit's feet, four-leaf clovers, leprechauns, finding pennies, walking under ladders, and black cats). Is there really "bad" or "good" luck? What can we say rather than wishing others "good luck"?

Explain: We don't need to worry about good or bad luck. We know God loves us and controls every part of our lives. Even if bad things happen, God tells us He will always be with us (Matthew 28:20). He also says He will make good things happen out of bad (Romans 8:28). Because God kept His promise to send a Savior, we know He really loves us and will keep His other promises too.

- **THANK** God for caring about every detail of our lives.
- **THANK** God for sending Jesus to be our Savior.
- **ASK** God to strengthen our trust in Him.

Box of Prayers

Read: Psalm 5:3

Do: Make a prayer box. Ask everyone to write prayers for meals, recess, tests, illness, etc. on index cards (one prayer per card). Decorate each card with stickers or colorful pictures. Place the cards in a recipe box. Make divider cards to separate the prayer cards into categories. Use the cards as applicable. Add to the box at regular intervals.

Explain: We can pray to God at anytime, for anything. God always wants to hear from us. He's always ready to listen. A prayer box can be a fun reminder to pray at mealtimes, before and after tests, and throughout the day. God will hear and answer our every request for Jesus' sake.

- **PRAISE** God for His answers to our prayers.
- **ASK** God to remind us to talk to Him throughout our day.
- **ASK** forgiveness for forgetting to talk to God.

Scripture Index